PRAISE FOR THE
Curious Encounters of the Human Kind
SERIES

"Most of Paul Sochaczewski's curious encounters start out as intelligent travel writing, exploring hidden corners of Asia and characters very much out of the ordinary. But this series works on a more complex level: he frequently zooms in and out of left field with a curious tangent, a sensitive reminiscence, a provocative opinion, a new way of looking at events that already are beyond most 'normal' travelers' tales. I read each story feeling refreshed, enlightened, and curious to see what the next stage of Sochaczewski's journey would bring."

—JUDITH M. HEIMANN, author of *The Most Offending Soul Alive: Tom Harrisson and His Remarkable Life* and *The Airmen and the Headhunters: A True Story of Lost Soldiers, Heroic Tribesmen and the Unlikeliest Rescue of World War II*

"What a discovery! Paul Sochaczewski is that rarest of writers who knows that the real 'Asian miracle' isn't malls or computer geeks. In his years traveling the continent, he has discovered an eternal assemblage of arcane explorers, putative emperors, frivolous mystics, sacrosanct elephants and, yes, miracle workers. When Sochaczewski finds them, in Javanese palaces or sacred forests protected by spirits, they are caviar (or sweetened bird's nest) for his fascinating portraits. A book for everyone who knows that the Mysterious East is alive and well, and more how-about-that-wonderful than you perhaps imagined."

—HARRY ROLNICK, author of *The Chinese Gourmet, The Complete Book of Coffee,* and *Spice Chronicles: Exotic Tales of a Hungry Traveler*

"Paul Sochaczewski skips about Asia like a Monkey God hopping from mountain to mountain, bringing back life-prolonging peaches while annoying the gatekeepers. Whatever you do, follow him on this journey!"

—LEE CHOR LIN, director of the National Museum of Singapore; former curator of Asian Civilizations Museum – Singapore; author of *Batik: Creating an Identity*

"Sochaczewski is a world-class searcher, reporter, and observer who has criss-crossed Asia for forty years, pausing in the most unlikely places and finding extraordinary people. The essays in this insightful and witty chronicle present a rich tapestry of eccentric nobles, self-serving naturalists, scoundrels who will make your teeth ache, celebrity monks, and memorable folks whose stories are too good to be true. But they are."

—CHRISTOPHER G. MOORE, author of the Vincent Calvino novels and *Heart Talk*

"In this series Sochaczewski explores the hidden corners, the forgotten people, and their surprising tales. All the personal traveler's tales in these volumes are captivating, all filled with humor, drama, and insight, with an edgy take-no-prisoners voice. You won't find anything else like this on the bookshelf."

—JEFF MCNEELY, chief scientist, International Union for Conservation of Nature

"The *Curious Encounters of the Human Kind* series is a delicious stew of improbable characters and intriguing stories, served up in thoroughly pithy style, and with a hearty dash of irreverent humour."

—TIM HANNIGAN, author of *Raffles and the British Invasion of Java* and *Brief History of Indonesia: Sultans, Spices, and Tsunamis: The Incredible Story of Southeast Asia's Largest Nation*

"Constructed on a base of strange but true personal travel adventures, *Curious Encounters* adds elements of history, an edgy sense of humour, mysticism, political incorrectness, current affairs, and memorable characters you'll wish you had the pleasure to meet on your travels. Consider each book in this series like a good curry – the result is more than the sum of its parts; each tale has its own zing. Travel with these books to the little-visited corners of Asia, and savour them.

—JASON BROOKE, director of The Brooke Trust

"I never tire of living vicariously through Paul Sochaczewski and his writing adventures. He keeps finding these wonderful details that miraculously open up entire worlds to be explored. Paul is the last of the Great Hunters, only instead of trophies, it is stories he brings home for our admiration, wonder, and delight."

—MARK OLSHAKER, Emmy-winning filmmaker;
author of *Einstein's Brain*, *The Edge*, and *Mindhunter*

"The *Curious Encounters* series is proof positive that a writer/ traveler can immerse himself in Asian cultures and yet remain objective enough to write extremely entertaining and often irreverent articles and colorful stories about what he has experienced. From Indonesian mystics to Burmese white elephant hunters, the descriptions are spot-on. There is something in these articles and stories that reminds me of the writing of Paul Theroux – not as cynical, perhaps, but the author is just as able to look at events with a clear, unsentimental and yet sympathetic eye. You won't regret a moment spent reading these tales, which perfectly capture the allure and spice of the places visited."

—DEAN BARRETT, author of *Memoirs of a Bangkok Warrior*

VOLUMES IN THE
Curious Encounters of the Human Kind
SERIES:

Myanmar (Burma)

Indonesia

Himalaya: India, Bhutan, Nepal

Borneo

Southeast Asia:
Thailand, Laos, Cambodia, Vietnam, the Philippines

OTHER TITLES BY PAUL SOCHACZEWSKI

Share Your Journey

An Inordinate Fondness for Beetles

The Sultan and the Mermaid Queen

Redheads

Distant Greens

Eco-Bluff Your Way to Greenism

Soul of the Tiger

CURIOUS

ENCOUNTERS

of the

HUMAN KIND

HIMALAYA

INDIA, BHUTAN & NEPAL

CURIOUS
ENCOUNTERS
of the
HUMAN KIND

HIMALAYA

True Asian Tales of
Folly, Greed, Ambition
and Dreams

PAUL SPENCER SOCHACZEWSKI

EXPLORER'S EYE PRESS

GENEVA, SWITZERLAND

Cover photo: Young girl by the roadside, Ladakh, India.

All photos by Paul Sochaczewski, except where noted.

Jeffrey McNeely contributed to an earlier version of "On the Yeti Trail."

ISBN: 978-2-940573-07-3

Published by:
Explorer's Eye Press
Geneva, Switzerland

Book design by Stacey Aaronson
Map of Himalaya by John Welding

Printed in the United States of America

*Dedicated to the people of Asia who shared their stories,
and sometimes their homes, rice wine, termite omelets,
and dreams.*

TABLE OF CONTENTS

AUTHOR'S NOTE

The Himalayan region brings out excessive giddiness in most travelers.

Maybe it's the presence of glaciers from which flow three of the world's most important rivers. It could be the admiration of armchair adventurers of the exploits of mountain climbers, surely among the most gifted sports people on Earth. Perhaps it's the hill tribes, or the elusive snow leopard and even harder-to-pin-down yeti. Maybe it's the altitude. It's probably not the food.

It's a place where geopolitics play hardball. Indian and Pakistani armed forces stare each other down at altitudes where breathing is almost impossible. For a while, Maoists ran roughshod in Nepal, and, proving that the Nepalese electorate can be as naïve as that in any other country, the Maoists were elected to form a hapless government. Three of the Himalayan countries featured in this book – India, Nepal, Bhutan – abut Tibet, and it's hard to find a more egregious example of arrogant colonialism than that of China toward Tibet, which it treats like a land of evil *tsampa*-eating bumpkins, home to red-robed people who need to be disciplined for imagined sins against the Middle Kingdom.

Roads, airstrips, and in Tibet's case, a high-speed railway, have improved communications somewhat, but quality education and healthcare remain, for the most part, luxuries of the lowlands.

And maybe that's what makes the Himalayas so attractive to visitors. People living in the high mountains go about their business as they see fit, retaining their culture in the face of various challenges. In more than a few cases the mountain forests are cut, the wildlife poached (China, again), the land mined for minerals, the rivers dammed. The climate, with its short growing season, does them no favors either.

It is a place where, more often than not, prayer flags unfurl. And, if you believe that the gods answer such prayers carried on the wind, then you might seek a retirement home in Shangri-La.

In a few instances the reader may find some statistics used in this volume outdated because several chapters, in simpler versions, have appeared over a period of twenty years in *The New York Times*, *International Herald Tribune*, *Wall Street Journal*, *Destinasian*, *GQ*, *CNN Traveller*, *Travel and Leisure*, *Geographical*, *Reader's Digest*, and other publications.

But while stats might change, the basic truth of the human stories offered here of foibles, ambitions, and achievements remains constant.

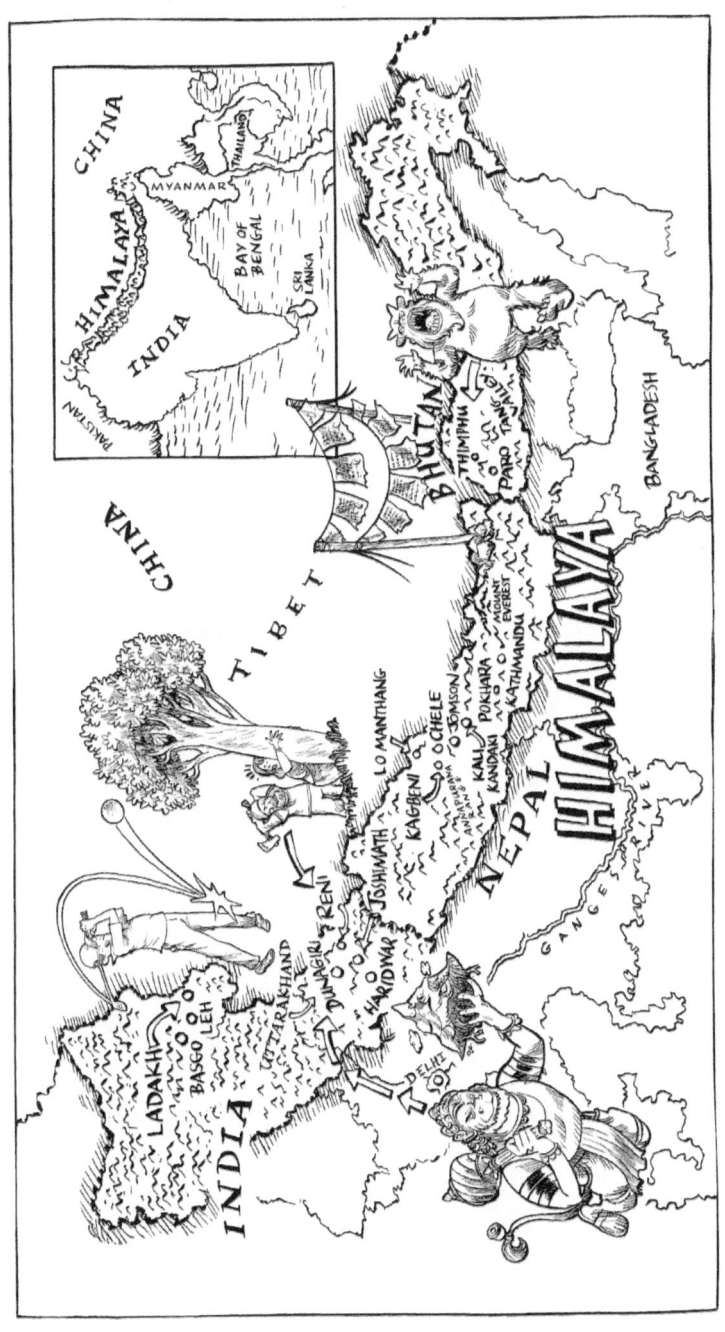

"You're looking for my daughter?"

THE GIRL BY THE
SIDE OF THE ROAD

Twenty-six years on, searching for the girl whose eyes said,
"I'm going to surprise you."

LADAKH, INDIA

In 1979 I took a black and white photo of a young girl in Ladakh. She was perhaps ten. She wore a rough robe of homespun wool, she carried a slate on which she used a stick dipped in muddy water to write her alphabets, and she carried a simple brown canvas army-style book bag slung over her shoulder.

I have no idea what she was thinking, but to me her gaze said, quietly, "Watch me. I'm going to surprise you."

I sought her out in April 2005.

There was a slight problem, though. I didn't remember where I had taken the photo.

One of the benefits of being a somewhat organized pack rat is that I keep my old journals. I found my notes from the trip twenty-six years earlier. At a town I had identified as Bongzo, I had written about a little girl whose "hands were rough with ingrained dirt, the texture of sandpaper." We had arithmetic as a common language, and I wrote "2 + 2" and watched her stroke the numeral "4." I gave her a ball point pen. "The girl's eyes lit for a moment with immediate recognition," I had written. "After realizing the pen was for her, she grabbed it and in one motion hid it inside her homespun robe."

In 2005 I was in the remote Himalayan region of Ladakh to write an article about the golf course in Leh, which at 3,445 meters is the world's highest. I had a free day, and understanding my esoteric interests, my guide, Tashi Chotak Lonchey, took me to the monastery I had visited twenty-six years earlier (yes, one of the monks was still alive and he recognized himself in a photo). After a cup of butter tea, we decided to drive several hours to visit a sacred forest, an ancient juniper tree grove in Hemis Shukpachan. En route, after driving for about an hour, we passed a small village and I saw a sign that said "Basgo."

"Maybe this is the place where you took the picture," Tashi suggested.

Bongzo? Basgo? Close enough to be worth a stop.

None of it looked familiar. My only thought was that in 1979 my friend David and I must have stopped here for a tea break during a bus ride to Ridzong Monastery further along the same road.

Tashi and I stopped at a large house near the road and showed a blowup of the young girl's photo to an old woman. "It could be Tsewang," she said after some thought. "Her husband Tashi Angchok is just up the street."

We found Tashi Angchok working at the family restaurant. He offered us tea as he studied the photo. "The smile looks similar to my wife's," he said. But the problem was that his wife, Tsewang Dolma, the reputed girl in the photo, wasn't around the day we stopped by since she teaches at Tridho, a one-class school some three hours away, near the Chinese border.

He took the picture to his mother-in-law and came back with a handful of old photos showing his wife as a young girl. The mother said that my photo seemed to be that of her daughter, but she wasn't too sure.

We still had a long program ahead of us that day, so we left the photo with Tashi Angchok, told him we would be back at the end of the afternoon, and went to explore the sacred forest in Hemis.

It was almost sundown when we got back to Basgo.

"It's her," Tashi said confidently.

We asked how he knew.

"I showed the picture to Tsewang's sister but didn't say 'is this Tsewang?' I simply asked, 'do you know this girl?'" he said, quite proud of his detective skills.

"She said 'yes, that's my little sister.'"

So, just like that I found a family who has invited me to dinner next time I'm in Ladakh. Then I'll get a chance to actually have a conversation with this girl, now a grown woman, whose photo and spirit has graced my home for a quarter of a century.

She wants her mountain back.

THE GOD WHO FLEW OFF
WITH A MOUNTAIN

*It takes chutzpah for an Indian villager to stay angry at
one of the most popular gods in the Hindu pantheon,
but Padhan Patti feels she has a good reason.*

DUNAGIRI, UTTANANCHAL, INDIA

t takes a chunk of Hindu chutzpah for a remote Indian villager to stay angry at one of the most popular gods in the pantheon, but Padhan Patti feels she has a good reason.

"When Lord Hanuman came here to retrieve the medicinal plant mountain, he promised to bring it back," the fifty-something woman says, referring to a pivotal scene in the classic Ramayana epic. "But he didn't." Padhan Patti promises that when I hike another few hours to a vantage point, I will see a huge "bleeding" scar on the side of Dunagiri mountain where the flying monkey god Hanuman is said to have sliced off a big chunk of mythological real estate.

Padhan Patti says she still respects Hanuman, the

flying monkey god, because after all he is the Hindu epitome of loyalty, devotion, and good works. Nevertheless, to register her disappointment in his lapse to keep his word, she refuses to take the *prasad*, or communion, at the village's annual Hanuman festival.

Clearly, Hanuman's role in the Ramayana is a story for the ages.

Having huge religious and cultural influence, with some of the story lines and moral impact of the Bible, the *Odyssey*, and the Ring Cycle, the Ramayana tells of how the wife of Indian Prince Rama (an avatar of Vishnu, one of the most powerful Hindu deities) is kidnapped by the ten-headed demon Ravana, who spirits the woman to his well-protected redoubt in his kingdom in what is now Sri Lanka. During the numerous battles that ensue, Lakshmana, Rama's devoted brother, is mortally wounded. The only thing that can save him is *sanjivani*, a combination of medicinal plants that only grow in the high Himalaya. The royal physician bemoans: "But we're stuck here in Sri Lanka and the plants grow up near the border with Tibet. Who we gonna call?"

This is when Hanuman comes to the rescue. The monkey god flies some 2,600 kilometers to the medicinal plant mountain, soaring at a speed of roughly 660 kilometers an hour, according to R.P. Goldman, from the University of California at Berkeley, who made his calculation based on the writings of ancient scholars. And then, depending on which of the many versions of the story you read, Hanuman either forgets which plants were on the shopping list or the plants hide in fear when they see this big monkey coming in for a landing. Either way, he rips up the mountain and carries it back to Sri Lanka. After one whiff of the healing herbs, Lakshmana is back in business, enabling him and his brother Rama to win the final battle, rescue Rama's wife Sita, and return home for a bittersweet finale. In most versions of the story, after the medicines have worked their magic, Hanuman puts the mountain back on his shoulder and flies again over the subcontinent to replace the crag in its rightful place.

HANUMAN'S SEARCH FOR HEALING PLANTS IN THE Himalaya has a basis in fact. Scientists and local people alike know well that the Himalayan region is a treasure chest of medicinal plants that comprise the heart of the Ayurvedic and other traditional medical systems used to treat Lakshmana, and which remain the treatments of choice for tens of millions of people in the region.

I WAS EXHAUSTED BUT THRILLED AS MY FRIEND GOPAL Sharma and I walked up the steep, narrow path to Dunagiri village. I've wanted to find Hanuman's mountain for some thirty years. Partly it was the quest for something that is inherently "unfindable," but I was also intrigued by an unintended side benefit. It is difficult to fly over a sub-continent carrying a mountain like a pizza delivery guy without bits of earth falling to the ground. Where these clumps of medicinal-plant dirt fell, sacred forests sprouted. These holy groves, places rich in healing herbs and generally protected by the local communities, can be found throughout Asia, and during my work in nature conservation I took a particular interest in their existence and the practical, cultural, and spiritual benefits such natural gardens provide to local people. How interesting it would be, I thought, to find the mother lode of these sacred forests.

Some people search for Mount Ararat, where Noah landed. Others seek Atlantis, or Solomon's temple, or the rumored companion city to Machu Picchu. I was searching for a mythical mountain from a story that provides entertainment and moral guidance for hundreds of millions of people.

But where was this elusive rock? I read dozens of books, spoke to a gaggle of scholars. Some Ramayana versions give poetically vague directions – "Go over the sea and north into the far high Himalaya. At night from the air you will easily see the glowing Medicine Hill of Life, crowned with herbs long ago transplanted from the Moon." Another version of the Ramayana places the medicinal-plant mountain between the (mythical) Rishabha mountain, full of fierce animals, and the (very real) Kailasa mountain, in Tibet. Yet another instructs Hanuman to fly nine thousand yojanas to the red mountain, then another nine thousand yojanas to the blue mountain, and on and on (Indian scholars who calculate such things

estimate that one ancient yojana is equal to approx-
imately thirteen to sixteen kilometers). N.C. Shah, of
the Central Council for Research in Indian Medicine in
Lucknow, pointed me toward Dunagiri by noting that
Hanuman's mountain was located "where *kshir*, or ocean,
was churned for *amrita*, ambrosia, and where existed two
hills, namely Chandra and Drona." An Indian conservation official said no, the mountain is in his home state
of Tamil Nadu, in the south of the country. More
prosaically, a friend in Mumbai asked, "Why are you
interested in this crazy goose chase in the first place?
No Starbucks in the mountains."

Eventually, Ajay Rastogi, a friend in Delhi with whom
I had worked during my tenure at the WWF – World Wide
Fund for Nature, said that he had heard about a village
where some folks refused to share in Hanuman's communion. Ajay couldn't make the trip, but he introduced me
to Gopal Sharma, a tough Indian mountaineer and
adventurer. Gopal Sharma had twice summited 7,817-
meter Nanda Devi (in one climb he survived a night
bivouacking without a sleeping bag at 7,600 meters, and
on another attempt survived a four-hundred-meter fall).

After a comfortable overnight train from Delhi to
Haridwar, a holy city where the Ganges leaves the
mountains and enters the plains, Gopal and I drove for
twelve hours to Joshimath, an Indian hill station in the
state of Uttaranchal that suffers from the ugly unregulated
construction and traffic of most such resorts. The next
morning, driving toward the border with China, we drove

another two hours to the trailhead, altitude 2,578 meters, in the general vicinity of the Nanda Devi Sanctuary.

I hike in the Alps on weekends and am no stranger to the mountains of India and Nepal, but I soon tired and huffed and puffed my way to our campsite at Dunagiri village at 3,651 meters, more than twice the height of Denver.

This was Ground Zero for my search. The hundred or so villagers in Dunagiri (the village, and the mountain of the same name, are sometimes referred to as Dronagiri) were curious, polite, and after a while quite willing to answer the strange questions of an out-of-breath foreigner. You can't see the 7,066-meter Dunagiri mountain from the village, and Gopal and I hiked up a few hundred meters to get a good view. We were lucky with the weather (on our departure a few days later it began to snow) and the permanently snow-topped mountain shone like a beacon. We clearly saw the gash where, one might imagine, part of the mountain had been sliced off.

I HAD MANY QUESTIONS I STILL WANTED TO ASK PADHAN Patti, but some queries ultimately could only be answered by Hanuman his divine self. This goal for an interview with Hanuman might not be so far-fetched, since in 2014 the BBC reported that an Indian postman named Heeralal Saini had tried, and failed, to deliver an official Indian biometric identity card in the name of Hanuman-Ji, son of

Pawan (Hanuman's father in mythology, the God of Wind, hence Hanuman's ability to fly). The identity card, number 2094705195411, included fingerprints and an iris scan, with a photo of Hanuman in full Ramayana regalia, wearing gold and pearl jewelry and a crown, with white whiskers decorating his simian face. The mobile phone number listed on the card did not connect. The government official in charge of the identity card program, which aims to issue an ID card to all of India's 1.2 billion citizens, called the hoax "a deliberate mischief." Perhaps. But equally plausible is that Hanuman, sensing our upside-down world needs his skills, has returned, the Indian equivalent of the USA's Superman who fought for "truth, justice, and the American way."

WE RETURNED TO THE VILLAGE TO SAY GOOD-BYE. I JUST wanted to be clear that I had the story right, and asked Padhan Patti to confirm that she really was upset with Hanuman because he didn't return the mountain. She nodded, but added a new fillip, another reason for being perturbed. She told the story with a familiarity and acceptance as if she was recounting a family tale that happened, say, a generation earlier, like my father's war stories. Hanuman flew in during a whiteout, she said, and couldn't find the mountain. Unlike most modern men he stopped to ask directions. The only person in the village was an old woman, an ancestor of Padhan Patti's. The old woman pointed in the direction Hanuman was to fly. "I can't see it and I'm in a hurry," Hanuman replied. So he put her on his shoulder and she navigated while he soared. They arrived, Hanuman said, "thanks, have a good life," grabbed the mountain and flew away, leaving the little old lady stranded in the middle of a blizzard.

HANUMAN'S PLANTS FACE UNCERTAIN FUTURE

In the meadows at the base of Hanuman's mountain, Gopal Sharma and I found one of the medicinal plants on Hanuman's shopping list, traditionally called *visalyakarani*, which in Sanskrit means "removing spikes and arrows." G.S. Rawat of the Wildlife Institute of India subsequently identified the plant as *Morina longifolia* (Dipsacaceae), used locally to heal wounds. Other herbal treatments Hanuman collected seem to have been mythical or generic concoctions containing hard-to-identify ingredients: *mritasanjivani* (resuscitating the dead), *suvarnakarani* (restoring strength to wounded limbs), and *sandhani* (curing fractures and cuts).

The Himalayan region is a treasure chest of important medicinal plants, which form the heart of the three-thousand-year-old Ayurvedic medical system. Ajay Rastogi, who started me on the quest for Hanuman's mountain, notes that many Indian

Himalayan medicinal plants are threatened because of habitat destruction and over-collection. In India, more than ninety-five percent of the four hundred medicinal plant species used in preparing medicines by various industries are harvested from the wild, according to Rana Man of the GB Pant Institute of Himalayan Environment and Development. In the Manali wildlife sanctuary in northwest India, with a similar mountain ecosystem to that of Dunagiri, Man recorded two hundred seventy medicinal plants, of which thirty-seven species were threatened because of over-collection.

And protect us from evil ...

꧁

FLYING PHALLUS FIGHTS FORCES OF EVIL

How does the male reproductive organ, "exuberant, slightly askew, and sometimes frothy," protect villagers?

NABJI, BHUTAN

"I can make you a new phallus, no problem."

"But we're leaving in the morning."

"Trust me."

Figuring that we could always use a bit more protection against demons in our house in Bangkok, I ordered a flying phallus sculpture from Karma, a village artist in central Bhutan.

This seemed to be a practical, and economical, form of Asian homeowners' insurance. Of course there was no guarantee that the wooden phallus, once imported to Thailand, would have the same anti-demon properties that it provides in this landlocked, traditional country, but I figured it was worth a ten-dollar investment.

After all, phalluses — sometimes simple and stylized, often ornate and anatomically correct — adorn many houses in Bhutan. And these phalluses must do a good job since Bhutan is famously pacifist, the people are largely content (this is the home of Gross National Happiness, after all), and the landlocked kingdom is relatively free of the troublesome domestic dramas that afflict other Asian countries.

Mind you, I already had an ample dose of good luck.

Our small group was trekking along the Nabji-Korphu Trail in the Jigme Singye Wangchuck National Park. Only a handful of trekkers are allowed to camp at each of the park's six campsites and we had the area virtually to ourselves. I spent hours sitting on a rock next to a river, watching electric blue kingfishers dart into the clear mountain water, alone in one of Asia's most interesting and beautiful protected areas.

But if a little good luck is nice, then surely lots of good luck and protection would be even better.

THROUGHOUT ASIA FOLKS RELY ON COSMIC BODY-guards that might come in the form of mystical tattoos, amulets, incantations, and making of merit.

The Bhutanese, however, choose the male repro-ductive organ to ensure that a home is free from evil spirits and slander.

These phallus images, called *po* in Dzonghka, Bhutan's national language, are sometimes painted on the outside walls of Bhutanese houses, sometimes carved from wood and hung from the eaves of their sturdy stone and timber dwellings. Dasho Karma Ura, head of the Center for

Bhutan Studies, describes these phalluses as "exuberant and gifted penises, always slightly askew and sometimes frothy."

The man who generally gets credited with popularizing the good-luck-phallus craze was a fifteenth- to sixteenth-century Buddhist yogi named Lama Drukpa Kunley. He was to phallus popularity what Brigitte Bardot was to the bikini.

Unlike the gentle and placid approach of mainstream Buddhist missionaries, Drukpa Kunley proselytized through anarchy, shock, and awe. He believed that only by spotlighting the absurdity of all fixed, man-made rules, and by forcing the student to abandon all ideas of predictability and emotional security, can people become wise enough to understand the "crazy wisdom" of Buddhist enlightenment.

Drukpa Kunley, *enfant terrible* of Buddhist missionaries, seducer of women (including his own mother, but it was for her own good, he argued), famously subdued the female demons of Bhutan with his "flaming thunderbolt." He exemplified the tantric belief that carnal relations can be the gateway to enlightenment, and was not hesitant to enlighten as many women as possible.

AS WE WERE FINISHING BREAKFAST THE FOLLOWING morning, Karma, the village artist, strolled into our camp with what appeared to be a colorful model airplane.

On closer examination we saw that he had carved a

pink-painted phallus as long as my forearm. To the business end of the phallus, Karma had added a strip of faded yellow cloth, perhaps an homage to the ubiquitous prayer flags found throughout the country, but more likely representing Anti-Demon Ejaculate. He had also carved a wooden sword, which he nailed at right angles to the phallus, giving the object the approximate look of a handmade, not quite completed B-52. Our friend and trekking guide Tashi Namgay explained that while the phallus provides protection, the wooden sword "cuts through ignorance, the first step toward wisdom."

My French wife dubbed it the "Flying *Zizi*", using the French slang for the male member.

We took our Flying *Zizi* to the simple village temple, set in the middle of a paddy field. We quickly located Dorji, a lay monk who doubled as the shrine's caretaker. He didn't flinch as we asked him to bless the object.

I asked Tashi, "This will work against all demons?"

"Actually, the really tough demons require something stronger," Tashi replied, his unwavering patience for our ridiculous questions tempered now with a hint of good-natured sarcasm.

"An extra large phallus, perhaps?"

"No, just the opposite. Naked dancing monks."

In reply to our perplexed looks, Tashi explained that this tiny village, a day's walk from the nearest road, was the epicenter for other significant phallus phenomena.

To simplify a complex legend, a group of devotees in Nabji had been trying to build a temple. Each day they would labor in the hot sun, and each night, as the workers slept, the mischievous anti-religious demons would tear down the holy structure. Finally, a monk named Dorje Lingpa led a nocturnal dance of naked men in order to distract the demons. The strategy worked, and eventually, following days of hot work and nights of cold dancing, the temple was built.

On our return to Thailand in May 2010, the people of Bangkok were tensing for a battle between rival Red Shirts and Yellow Shirts. A military intervention seemed certain, and just a kilometer away armed soldiers were gathering for a final showdown with the implacable demonstrators.

We carefully unpacked our Flying *Zizi* and hung it in our Thai garden. "This will work in Bangkok?" I had asked Karma when we purchased the talisman.

That kind of question may have been a touch too abstract for Karma, a village boy who had never even been to the Bhutanese capital of Thimphu. But the shrug he gave us seemed to say, "can't hurt."

And he was right. While central Bangkok burned, life on our little *soi* continued relatively undisturbed. The noodle guy in front of our house stayed open, as did the grilled chicken lady, the vegetable seller, and the motor-cycle-taxi drivers. The cat slept peacefully. I'm not too sure that the sword helped us to cut through ignorance to achieve wisdom, but I'm pretty certain that at least the phallus-fearing demons went elsewhere.

Tashi's philosophy:
"The more you help people now,
the better it will be in the next life."

LIFE: ENDLESS KARMIC LOOP OR SOLE CHANCE FOR GUSTO?

A friend returns to his birthplace on the Tibetan plateau to chase demons and seek cosmic explanations.

LO MANTHANG, MUSTANG, NEPAL

n a bluff in Kagbeni, at the entrance to the Kingdom of Mustang, a tantalizing sign warns: "Stop. You are now entering the restricted area of Upper Mustang."

Our vantage point in this medieval-feeling town overlooks the Kali Gandaki River. We look up the wide, graveled riverbed toward distant villages, where patches of green barley offer evidence of civilization in this arid landscape. We gaze at the ancient Salt Route that winds along the river's banks. The track, accessible only by foot, pony, or yak, connects the lowlands of India and Nepal with the isolated mountain plateaux of Central Asia. Before we can enter Upper Mustang, we first must show our trekking permits to the Nepalese authorities. Then we are through, and it feels like we have entered a hidden

Narnia-like gate, a forbidden time warp. The snow-capped peak of Nilgiri Mountain, part of the Annapurna range, is at our backs. We are headed north, toward Tibet.

***

FOR THE THREE WESTERNERS IN OUR GROUP, THE TREK to the Kingdom of Mustang in northern Nepal is the start of an adventure to a seldom visited, exotic land.

For Tashi, however, it is an emotional homecoming.

Our friend Tashi, a smiling, stocky Tibetan refugee who became a naturalized Nepalese citizen, was born some forty years earlier in a nameless valley near Lo Manthang, the capital of Upper Mustang and our destination five days hence.

His family, from the Saga region in southwestern Tibet, escaped in 1958, just before the Chinese invasion. Nomadic shepherds, they wandered with their flocks of yaks, sheep, and goats in the brown and ochre high-altitude deserts of Mustang.

We hope to arrive for the beginning of the annual Tiji festival, a three-day exorcism to rid the world of devils.

Tashi has never seen Tiji. He has never returned to his birthplace.

***

THE REASON FOR UPPER MUSTANG'S ISOLATION IS partly physical, and mostly geopolitical. Following the Dalai Lama's flight from Tibet to India in 1959, a band of

Tibetan guerrillas used Mustang as their center of anti-Chinese operations (Lo Manthang is just twenty-five kilometers from the border). To quell the uprising, the Chinese closed the Tibet-Mustang border in 1960 and pressured the Nepalese government to seal off Mustang from the rest of Nepal.

While a handful of researchers were allowed into the area, Mustang remained virtually closed to foreigners until March 1992. The government of Nepal, experimenting with a newly democratic outlook and eager to generate foreign exchange, decided that up to a thousand people a year could visit this isolated region.

A great part of Mustang's appeal to foreigners, of course, lies in the fact that it is hard to get to. There are no roads, no cars, no mountain bikes. A visitor walks, rides a pony, or charters a helicopter.

The other element of the appeal is that Mustang is perhaps the best place in the world to get close to Tibetan culture. Mysterious Tibet. Something about Tibet appeals to Westerners' longing for places that are dramatically different, especially when the esoteric culture, traditions, and history are complemented by a religion that preaches non-violence, worries about karma, and enthusiastically believes in masked battles between the forces of good and evil.

WHAT IS IT THAT ATTRACTS PEOPLE TO THINGS "forbidden"?

Our natural curiosity? A self-testing? The desire to get away from our routine lives and see what kind of steel we have inside us?

We exert a bit of physical effort to hike these trails.

The walking is strenuous, made tougher by the afternoon dust storms that originate in the lowlands and roar through the narrow Himalayan passes.

We suffer a bit – blisters, fatigue, the broken ribs of my friend Didier – but when we spend too much time complaining about grit in our eyes, we are pulled back to reality by remembering the epic crises recounted by Jon Krakauer in his book *Into Thin Air*. This account of the disastrous 1996 climbing season on Mount Everest includes the tale of Beck Weathers, a Texan climber who was several times given up for dead and abandoned outside in blizzards on the top of the world. Virtually blind, with severe frostbite (his nose had to be amputated, along with his right arm, the four fingers and thumb of his left hand, and parts of both feet), he somehow stumbled into camp, a frigid, immobile, unseeing ghost of a man. His refusal to die made our aches not worth complaining about.

I appreciate travel more when I have to push myself physically. Clears my mind. And, in a way, any strenuous journey (and I use the term to include spiritual and emotional travel) is a way of leaving home.

Bruce Chatwin suggested that "'travel' is the same word as 'travail,' bodily or mental labor, toil, especially of a painful or oppressive nature, exertion, hardship, suffering, a journey."

We travel to test ourselves. To cleanse, to rejuvenate. According to Chatwin, "this could be termed 'catharsis,' which is Greek for purging or cleansing." He notes that one controversial etymology of the word derives from the Greek *katheiro*, to rid the land of monsters.

It made complete sense to arrive for Tiji and its casting out of demons.

IN ADDITION TO A MAJOR EXPENDITURE OF "TOIL," entering the "forbidden" kingdom requires a big chunk of cash.

The flimsy green trekking permit to cross the border into Upper Mustang costs seventy dollars per day, with a ten-day minimum. In addition, our little group had to pay a substantial sum for the trek itself, and then cough up another four hundred dollars to cover the costs of the mandatory liaison officer. Our liaison officer, Sharma, always immaculately dressed and coifed, always ready with a smile, is a mid-level official from the Nepal immigration department who came along mainly to make sure that we didn't walk past Lo Manthang and into Tibet itself. Every trekker I met along the route grumbled about this unnecessary, expensive, and cumbersome requirement. But if that's the price to pay to get into this special land, so be it.

The seven hundred dollar mandatory fee has led to considerable tension in Upper Mustang.

Purna Kunwar, the Jomson-based director of ACAP –

Annapurna Conservation Area Project – an NGO that runs many of the development projects in the Annapurna region, explained the situation.

"When the government opened up Mustang to tourists in 1992, they signed an agreement with ACAP promising that sixty percent of the fee would go for development in Upper Mustang," he said.

That would have been a nice sum, based on potential income from the eight hundred visitors who enter Upper Mustang annually.

In practice, Kunwar explained, the amount allocated is just eight percent, totalling about forty-five hundred dollars, which doesn't go very far when shared by a dozen villages spread over two thousand square kilometers.

In 1998 the local Tiji organizing committee hit tourists with a hefty camera fee of fifty dollars per day for a still camera, and one hundred and fifty dollars per day for a video (on top of a different five-hundred-dollar video camera fee that was to be paid in Kagbeni). Their rationale was that they needed the cash to maintain the costumes, instruments, and paintings used in the Tiji festival.

This fee was announced in a paper handed out to visitors when they first dug their Nikons out of their backpacks. "Hearty welcome to Teeji Festival," it read. "Owing to our lenience towards clicking the festival in the preceding years its deep rooted religious festival gets diluted which in turn decreases the number of its attendants as it had before."

Pema Tsering, 30, a shy, articulate teacher at the Great Sakyapa Monastic School and spokesman for the Tiji festival committee explained:

> We're embarrassed by this as well. But what can we do? Most of the little money that ACAP collects for Upper Mustang goes for community development. Almost nothing is allocated for cultural development. We use this income to maintain the Tiji costumes. We've asked the government for some money but they ignore our request. If we don't take the initiative the government certainly won't do it for us.

The committee raised about fifteen hundred dollars from camera fees paid by fifteen tourists.

Most tourist groups nominated a designated photographer and bought one pass. One American doctor from Milwaukee, Wisconsin, had his video camera confiscated (it was returned to him when he left Lo Manthang) by Tiji camera spies who busted him when he ignored the fine print in the festival's letter: "Severe action will be taken by the committee for those who are seen clicking without permits and who violate this rule in any unfair and tricky means."

TIJI SEEMED A FINE OPPORTUNITY TO DISCUSS philosophy.

"Tashi," I asked. "What's the meaning of life?"

Tashi is a Tibetan Buddhist. For him, life is a series of

nearly endless loops, where your past ungraceful actions generally come back to haunt you.

He explained his spiritual operating system. "Do whatever you can according to your capability. The more you help people now, the better it will be in the next life. Believe in God. Meditate."

"Tashi, you're making it too complicated," I replied. "Basically life really is a beer commercial. You're only sure of going around once, so make the most of it."

But Buddhists, like the followers of so many other religions, believe that life is suffering. It's the Vince Lombardi school of religion – "no pain, no gain."

"Tashi, let me tell you the philosophy of the North American baby-boom tribe," I said. "Nobody on his death bed ever said, 'Gee, I wish I had stayed later in the office and made love less.'"

He responds with an aphorism. "You plant rice, you get rice."

TASHI AND I WATCHED THE TIJI DANCES. TO ME IT WAS simply a glorious spectacle. We watched monks clad in golden silk brocade robes, peaked leather hats, and yak-hair boots don masks to enact the convoluted drama – part morality play, part epic. It was a bit like watching the Ring Cycle – some spectacular moments mixed in with some tedious half hours. Some monks tooted three-meter-long copper trumpets and clanged cymbals against a background of a giant *thanka* (religious painting) that hangs in the town square and is half the size of a tennis court. The noise and dust gives a feeling of a Tibetan country fair with touches of *commedia dell'arte*.

To Tashi, though, the events were sacred and profound.

The objective of Tiji is peace and brotherhood. Evil spirits are told to get out of town, and if the dancing monks have done their jobs properly, the demons will have been effectively banned until next year's festival.

TASHI HAS HIS OWN DEMONS TO DEAL WITH.

He was stateless and lived much of his early life in refugee camps. He never went beyond the ninth grade. And, the toughest karma of all, his son has cerebral palsy.

I ask him whether anything can be done to help the boy.

"It's our karma," he explains. "My wife and I might have done bad things in a previous life, and our son might have done worse things."

Tashi explains that he went to see the Dalai Lama's doctor in Dharamsala, India, who confirmed a diagnosis of bad karma, but nevertheless suggested that the boy take some medicine. The karma, in this case, was stronger than the herbs, and the boy is still wheelchair bound, unable to do anything for himself.

"You know, Tashi, all these religions and philosophies that predict some kind of next-world reward calculated on how many karma points you earn now are based on a big gamble," I said. "The only things you can be really sure about are that today you're alive and one day you won't be. Therefore, following the Cartesian logic of Anheuser Busch, the patron saint of fraternities, grab all the gusto you can while your plumbing's intact and before Alzheimer's sets in."

Being Asian and too polite to sneer, he pretended to think about it for a while.

I REFLECTED TOO. ON THE TRAIL A FEW DAYS EARLIER we had stopped by the settlement of Gheling. By the village well, where the water wheel was carved like a prayer wheel and carried offerings to heaven with each squeaky turn, we glimpsed a shy, disfigured girl.

We asked about her and that night her father brought her to the house where we were staying. Her name was Tashi Angmo. Several years ago a *dzo* spiked her in the eye with his horn. The wound was never treated, and her face became infected and ugly.

Poor and healthy is tough. Poor and disfigured is *really* tough karma. But who were we to interfere?

We asked the father why he hadn't sought medical help for the girl. With his daughter observing from the corner of the smoky room, he explained that they were poor and he had many children and anyway there weren't any doctors nearby. With Tashi Gurung's help, we channeled a few hundred dollars through a local non-governmental organization; Tashi Angmo left her village for the first time and was brought to distant Kathmandu for surgery. Our hope was that she would be able to see out of the eye and maybe have a shot at a relatively normal life. Was it her karma to get gored by a *dzo*? Was it her karma for us to trek into her village while she was washing the family's clothes?

LO MANTHANG IS A THIRD RATE SHANGRI-LA. IT IS A walled city, but because Raja Jigme Palbar Bista (the twenty-fifth king in a line of succession founded in 1380) has given permission for people to build outside the city limits, the town's fortress-like character has been modified. The streets and drains are shared by people, dogs, donkeys, and yaks. Although there are public standpipes bringing in clean water, little children drink from the open drains. Dust permeates our clothes. The king's palace is a ramshackle affair, in need of an overhaul. Lo Manthang has been without its hydro-generated electricity for several years. No one is quite sure why, but basically something has broken and no one has bothered to fix it. There is talk of constructing an airstrip, but no one expects it to happen soon. Medical care is basic – people with serious illnesses have to be carried to Jomson, eighty-seven kilometers away, then flown to Pokhara or Kathmandu.

The flat stucco roofs are perfect places to dry yak dung, firewood, and thorny kindling, piles of which make fine nesting sites for finches. The three-story houses are as mysterious as the town itself, with narrow passageways and tiny hidden stairwells. The houses often have a large central courtyard, with rooms facing inward, resembling the inns featured in Chinese sword-fighting movies. It would be a great place to shoot a James Bond action movie.

The people of Upper Mustang are isolated, but they are not naïve. In the summer they farm and herd livestock, but in the winter they wander far and seek new sights. Many people travel to India, where they successfully trade in woolen goods and cheap acrylic sweaters. Some shepherds head north into Tibet to trade sheep for Chinese goods. The donkey and yak caravans of the old Salt Route now carry a modest selection of manufactured goods, and at the Tiji festival the children showed off their ability to blow big pink bubbles with their Dubble Bubble chewing gum. Most young men of Lo Manthang sported made-in-China counterfeit baseball caps of American sports teams – the Chicago Bulls, the New York Yankees, the Miami Heat, the San Francisco Giants.

THIS BUSINESS OF KARMA KEPT COMING BACK TO ME.

Tashi runs a charity called the Himalayan Children's Foundation, which helps young Tibetan refugees get a good education. Through this group I sponsor the education of Tsering Wangmo, an 11-year-old Tibetan refugee girl.

She's a great kid. Bright eyes, a little shy, cute as Bambi.

Once she wrote me a poem:

"King love Queen
Queen love baby
Baby love milk
But I love you."

More recently, showing off a bit, she wrote: "Please don't angry if there is some mistake in my letter and if my handwriting is bad. But I don't think that there is some mistake and handwriting is bad because no[w] I am 6 class."

Was it her karma to meet me through Tashi and get the education that might lead to a more successful life? Was it my karma to meet Tashi when two Canadian friends stopped by my Switzerland house one morning and invited me to go on a bike ride with this friendly man from distant mountains? Was it Tashi's karma to have a handicapped son and to devote his life to helping others?

Tashi had no doubts about his belief. "If you do good things you will get good things," he said.

Tashi collects karma points the way some people collect baseball cards. His version of karma implies a system of bonuses and penalties.

But I'm not sure anyone's keeping score. All I know is that synchronicity, to use Jung's term, is real. We met, after all.

I don't claim to understand much of this, but I accept it. In my wallet I had Tsering Wangmo's latest letter. "Many years gone I will be a good and best and intelligent girl in the world. That's all for today." She signed it: "I never forgot your kindness until you die."

YEARS LATER, THIS BUSINESS OF KARMA KEEPS REAPPEARING.

Tsering Wangmo, my adopted daughter from Nepal, immigrated to the United States when her family won the green card lottery. They live in a cramped windowless basement apartment in Queens, New York, which is the most culturally diverse urban area in the world – I recall a factoid that some one hundred sixty nationalities live along the number 7 subway line. Tsering's parents got union jobs as housekeepers at the Hilton Hotel in midtown Manhattan, which guarantees a living wage, health care, and some social life with other people in New York – some, like them, just trying to get by in a new country. Tsering herself works as an administrator for a large New York hospital and is completing her bachelor's degree in hospital management.

And Tashi Angmo, the village girl whose eye was damaged by a yak? In 2015 I asked a friend, who happens to be an expert on the art and culture of Upper Mustang, to stop by Gheling village when he next visited the region. He easily found Tashi Angmo's family, who explained that she had become a Buddhist nun and is now studying at the Central University of Tibetan Studies in Varanasi, India. My friend obtained her email address (isn't globalization wonderful?) and I sent her a note. Six hours later she replied. She explained that at the request of her teacher she has changed her name to Ngawang Dechen and studies languages and Buddhist philosophy. She enjoys reading and has friends and purpose. She sent a few selfies – her face is unscarred and her eyes bright with life. I suspect she has much to teach me.

BEFORE WE ENTER LO MANTHANG WE STAND ON A HILL, looking at the centuries-old town that had required so much effort to reach. The late afternoon windstorm is blowing sand into our faces and we protect ourselves with white prayer shawls. Lo Manthang appears to be a mirage that might disappear if we proceed.

"I can see now the kind of life my parents had," Tashi explains. "They had hard karma. Many obstacles to overcome."

On the afternoon of the third and final day of Tiji, the dancers leave Lo Manthang through the town's sole entrance gate, followed by several hundred people from Lo Manthang and surrounding villages and a sprinkling of tourists. At dusk, courtiers fire ancient muskets as a high lama shoots arrows at a puppet representing a demon. This is an important moment for the star Tiji dancer, Lama Nag Kunga, who meditated in isolation for three months prior to Tiji in order to purify his soul and obtain the inner strength needed to cast the demons out of this place. He's doing his best to ensure a better future for mankind.

The moment is oddly profane and sacred at the same time. I glance at Tashi, thirty meters away, who watches intently. I don't disturb him.

Sending a message to eco-bureaucrats.

PRⱯYER FLⱯGS OVER RIO

*Should we trust the international bureaucrats
or the farmer in Bhutan for eco-solutions?*

JANGTSIKHA, BHUTAN

 was cleaning up my office and stubbed my toe against the printed version of *Agenda 21*, some seven hundred pages containing 2,079 recommendations, guidelines, and treaties resulting from the 1992 Earth Summit in Rio – the largest eco-bureaucratic gathering ever held. I hefted the volume to my desk and felt tired just reading the table of contents. All that political energy, all that money. All that effort aimed at saving the world. But it's hard to keep a party going. In spite of hundreds of major international conferences scheduled since Rio to encourage follow-up, the environment seems to have been usurped as everyone's favorite cause by the economy, the economy, and the economy.

I remember where I was during the Earth Summit. I had elected to look for an environmental experience instead of bathing in Rio's environmental spectacle. I spent Earth Summit week sitting on top of a mountain in

Bhutan while the leaders of just about every country on the planet gathered in Rio to figure out how to save the world. When I think of the Rio conference, an image of a Bhutanese farmer named Gyeltsnen comes to mind.

The diverse mixture of diplomats and eco-activists who gathered in Rio (including a Bhutanese delegation that was led by the king's sister) were looking at the big picture and posturing for the small screen. These men and women debated serious issues. Global trade patterns. Sustainable development. Transfer of technology. How to move big bucks from the people who have them to the people who don't. How to appear selfless to the press while nevertheless getting what they, and their consti- tuents back home, really want. Eco-politics, enhanced with more than a little eco-babble.

My aerie perch overlooked a Buddhist *dzong*. The air was thin at forty-two hundred meters, and my synapses performed cosmic helicopter whirls. Prayer flags blew in the wind. While people met in Rio I looked down on a valley perhaps two kilometers wide and eight kilometers long. I counted three houses. I saw nothing but trees blanketing the hills.

I'd guess that there can't be more than several hundred Bhutanese who were aware that the world's most important eco-conference was being held that week. The rest of the country's people live and will likely die without recognizing the importance to their well-being of eco- bureaucrats strolling along Ipanema and Copacabana.

During Rio week I descended fifteen hundred meters

and visited Jangtsikha village, where I had a discussion with a farmer. His name was Gyeltsnen. It was very Aristotlean. He looked at my Swiss Army knife, my French backpack, my Italian trekking shoes, my American tent, my Australian pants with zippers at the knees to turn them into shorts. He concluded, as any sensible person from a developing country would, that I was rich. It took him no time at all to point out that the reverse was also true. He was wearing woolen homespun, he could write no language and could speak only one, his family's most important possessions were six cattle, assorted pigs and chickens, a house he had inherited from his ancestors, and his wife's turquoise jewelry. He therefore concluded, sensibly, that he was poor.

"You're wrong. You're not poor at all. You're rich," I said provocatively. Gyeltsnen looked skeptical. "You are totally self-sufficient," I argued with Euro-pragmatism. "Not to mention the fact that the king provides your family with free medical care and your children with free schooling."

Gyeltsnen did not look convinced.

"You are totally self-sufficient," I repeated. "If there's ever a global war, it's guys like you who will survive."

Gyeltsnen said nothing.

"And the most important things are all around you," I said, waving my arms. It was easy to get carried away in Bhutan's pine-scented hills. This is roughly what I said: "You have the most important things anyone can have. Because you've got forests you've got clean, fresh water.

You've got a set of spiritual beliefs that provides psychological support for however many lives you may have. You have built-in conservation safeguards – you yourself just told me that the tree we're sitting under is sacred. And you've got a family that stays together. People in the west don't have those things any more. This forest and these prayer flags and these children make you a rich man."

"You can afford to travel to Bhutan," Gyeltsnen said with finality. "I cannot travel to visit you."

I had no answer for him. And I'm sure that he probably wasn't convinced that he was richer than most other people. No, the only way to show the people of Bhutan how rich they are will be to bus them over to Nepal so they can see how some nineteen million people have wiped out their own forests, how without forests the Nepalese are forced to endure regular landslides, how they suffer a chronic shortage of firewood and clean water. The *coup de grace* would be to show him what critics call "tourists' prayer flags," a euphemism that describes colorful strips of used toilet tissue adorning the most popular trekking routes. He would see how the Nepalese have modified their traditional cultures of Hinduism and Buddhism in order to accommodate a third religion, Tourism. How farmers can't grow very many crops in the denuded hills and how urbanites can't breathe in the Nepalese capital Kathmandu.

Bhutan is an economic anomaly, and it would be wrong to assume that all is well. It's dangerous and naïve to overly praise Bhutan. The country has problems, to be sure – people and wildlife conflicts, young people leaving the farms to move to the capital, lack of jobs for an increasingly educated population, and the very beginning of previously unheard of social problems like prostitution and drug use. Based on statistics like GNP per capita ($425), low life expectancy at birth (48.9 years), adult literacy (30%), and numbers of doctors in the country (42 in 1988), Bhutan lies in the bottom third on the UN's list of countries. It also has a long way to go in the technology sweepstakes – two hundred eighty-five people per telephone, compared to say ten people per phone in Brazil. Yet in terms of nature it's in pretty good shape. Bhutan maintains, by Royal decree, sixty percent of its land as forests. Protected areas cover twenty percent of the country's surface. These forests provide water, but riches like regular clean water are rarely factored into the UN lists that judge how well off a country might be.

Famously, Bhutanese leaders have created, internalized, and promoted a national philosophy called Gross National Happiness. Because there are only six hundred thousand people in this Switzerland-sized kingdom, and because the king's word is law, and because outside cultural and trade influence is tightly restricted (a maximum of four thousand tourists are allowed in annually; they must pay two hundred fifty dollars a day for the privilege), and because the government is fiscally cautious (positive foreign exchange reserves, no debt, balanced budget), this land the people call "Land of the Thunder Dragon" may continue to go its own rhododendron-blessed way.

How many other countries represented at the Rio Earth Summit have such a wealth of nature? Up here on the hill I can think of perhaps just a dozen nations that haven't trashed their natural heritage like a rental car. Maybe it doesn't matter that Bhutan's national airline has just one plane that flies into a single airport. Like a pretty girl chooses her suitors, Bhutan picks and chooses the foreign aid agencies with which it wants to deal. Like a legendary princess, Bhutan lives in splendid isolation, a land where there is no democracy but where every subject can request an audience with the king. Like a wise man, Bhutan has decided, for the moment at least, to make friends carefully and not base its behavior on greed.

How does a country value its wealth? If I were an economist, I'd point out that GNP statistics mean little unless you have the vision to recognize that Bhutan has trees as far as the eye can see. Then I'd add a point that many economists would miss. There are prayer flags here that catch the clean wind and send messages to places most Rio-delegates have never dreamed of.

BLUFF YOUR WAY TO SAVING THE EARTH

About the time eco-bureaucrats met in Rio – while I was hiking up a Bhutanese mountain – politicians, businesspeople, taxpayers, journalists, and hucksters were in the flush of an eco-revolution.

Green had become the world's trendiest color, and many people, it seemed, wanted to either learn about conservation or, if that was too much trouble, at least appear to be concerned. Sensing a marketing opportuity as much as wanting to perform a public service, Jeff McNeely and I wrote *Eco-Bluff Your Way to Instant Environmental Credibility*. Our logic was that it's a lot of trouble, not to say depressing, to really dig into environmental issues. We argued that an hour spent with our book would give the reader enough clever factoids, memorable anecdotes, and handy jargon to impress potential dates and get lucrative consulting gigs.

Depressingly, many of the issues (destruction of tropical rainforests, loss of biodiversity, self-serving conservation groups, wildlife trafficking, hypocritical politicians, greenwashing businesses, corrosive lobbyists, overpopulation, polluting heavy industries, modern-day colonial attitudes) highlighted in the book are still with us. Sure, a few new problems (climate change, fracking, genetic engineering, ocean acidification) have arisen, but lord help us. *Plus ça change ...*

Hug a tree like your life depends on it.

TO CUT THAT TREE,
CUT THROUGH ME

Chipko women's movement keeps on huggin'.

RENI, UTTARANCHAL, INDIA

ny New-Age nature lover can hug a tree, and many do. But it takes a special kind of person to embrace a tree that is about to be chopped down and challenge the woodsman by saying, "If you want to cut this tree, you'll have to cut through me."

The Chipko movement in north India was founded on this kind of dare.

I met Srimati Bali Devi Rana, a leader of this unstructured movement, at her two-hundred-ten-person village of Reni, about an hour above the Indian hill station of Joshimath in the state of Uttaranchal.

Sitting on the roof of her two-story house, with hay drying at our feet and tall peaks just a few kilometers away, she welcomed me with cold clear water and homemade nibbles made of corn flakes, peanuts, and masala. Srimati, an animated woman wearing an orange woolen head scarf and homespun jacket and shirt, ran me through the historical origins of the movement.

Around 1730, people of the Bishnoi community in Rajasthan tried to protect their community forests by hugging the trees; some three hundred sixty-three people were killed by soldiers. On hearing of the massacre, the Maharaja of Jodhpur ordered timber cutting to stop.

That action established the principle that tree hugging is a viable but sometimes bloody way to protect local forests. Tree hugging as a social movement became as Indian as *chapati* and *dhal*. And the need to protect trees grew more and more urgent as India's population grew, new roads opened previously inaccessible regions to exploitation, and people in the lowland cities saw that there was considerable money to be made by exploiting the forests.

Nevertheless, mountain folks argued that the forests were their sole source of livelihood, since the rough terrain and short growing season prevented significant agriculture. Because of this conflict, the Chipko movement sprang up again in April 1973. Basically the local people wanted control over their forests.

This situation festered and finally exploded when the local village commune set up to run forest-product industries was denied its annual quota of ash trees that they used to manufacture farming tools; the government instead gave the logging rights to a large "foreign" manufacturer of sporting goods.

The villagers were incensed by this disregard of their

traditional rights and loss of an important income source.

Srimati explained that the forest contractor sent in two hundred axemen one evening when the contractor knew that most of the village men had gone into the town to collect seasonal compensation from the district headquarters. "Two of our women, who had gone down to the river to collect water, saw these forest laborers going up and quickly informed and alerted the rest of us," Srimati said. "All the women decided that, even in the absence of men, we had to act on our own to try to stop those laborers from cutting trees."

The women confronted the contractor's axemen and tried to talk them out of it. When that failed, the women rushed to protect the trees, "embracing them as children," and challenged the contractors to swing their axes against the villagers' backs.

That protest, and subsequent actions, led to a major victory in 1980 with a fifteen-year ban on tree cutting in the Himalayan forests of Uttar Pradesh, by order of India's then prime minister, Indira Gandhi. The movement later spread to other states and helped force government officials to focus on the need for natural resource policies that were more sensitive to people's needs.

Srimati, who is the head of the Mahila Mangal Dal (Women's Welfare Group) in northern India, offered me fresh slices of cucumber and homemade biscuits. I told her about my first contact with Chipko, which is a Hindi word meaning "stick to" or "cling" – not "hugging" as the feel-good Western translation puts it.

During the mid-1980s, while I was working for WWF in Switzerland, I was asked to show an Indian visitor the sights. More than a few heads turned as Sunderlal Bahuguna, slight, much-bearded, and wearing a colorless woolen homespun robe a la Mahatma Gandhi embraced a several-hundred-year-old oak tree near the Chateau de Nyon. In his deep Indian accent, he explained how the women of northern India had started Chipko in order to protest against the deforestation that was threatening their livelihood. Bahuguna, a seemingly humble man, alluded that his five-thousand-kilometer trans-Himalayan protest march and appeal to Indira Gandhi resulted in a ban on tree-felling. He was visiting Switzerland to seek international support to stop the Tehri dam in the Himalayan region. Bahuguna claimed that people "butcher the earth," and he railed against "suicidal activities being carried out in the name of development." He gave me a new perspective on nature conservation, introducing me to the power of emotional, culturally specific campaigns enacted by the people most affected by environmental damage. At the same time, I wondered why the international face of a woman's movement was that of a man.

As I reminisced about my favorable impressions of Bahaguna, who had introduced me to such tantalizing concepts, Srimati Bali Devi Rana interrupted me.

"Sunderlal Bahuguna is a thief," she exclaimed. Taken aback by such voluble emotion from a pleasant Asian woman I had just met, I asked her to explain her accusation. "Sunderlal Bahuguna was a contractor who cut the trees and made a lot of money," she explained. "After he got rich, he claimed he had a change of heart and declared he was part of the movement."

Obviously passions run high when trees meet politics.

When I visited Reni village, Srimati had just returned from Nairobi, where she had received a UNEP award and spoken at an international conservation conference, sharing the stage with Kenyan Nobel peace laureate Wangari Maathai. It was the first trip outside India for the fifty-seven-year-old woman, a voyage no doubt made more than a little challenging since she speaks no English. I pointed out that Chipko is famous around the world. Did that make her proud?

Not particularly, she decided. "Lots of learned people come here to write scholarly papers about our idyllic life," she said, "but they live in cities that are dirty." She thought a moment. "We don't write our literature. Our literature is the mountains, the jungles, the animals, and holy spirits. People come to see our literature."

Plenty of opportunity for golf next time around?

FIRE ΛND FURY ΜIGHT HΛVE TO WΛIT FOR THE NEXT LIFETIΜE

The Indian Army controls the world's highest golf course,
bringing a surprising set of challenges.

LADAKH, INDIA

thought it might be the altitude that would get to me, but it turned out to be military bureaucracy.

Since my first visit in 1979, I had wanted to play golf in Ladakh, an isolated corner of northern India that forms part of the high-altitude Tibetan plateau. I wasn't particularly interested in golf during that visit three decades earlier, but nevertheless I vividly remembered the sight of black-sand "greens" sitting amidst an ochre-colored wasteland. The sight appealed to my sense of the ridiculous. What was a golf course doing up there in a land of Tibetan monks, yaks, and oxygen-deficient atmosphere?

But the altitude, 3,445 meters, where climbing a flight of stairs felt to me like Tenzing's and Hillary's struggle to the summit of Everest, turned out to be a non-factor. I had underestimated that classic oxymoron – military intelligence.

Since my first visit to Ladakh I became a golf junkie,

and when I visited India's capital Delhi on business, I made some calls to see what it would take to play in Ladakh.

"Yes, there is a course," a well-placed friend, himself a retired officer, advised. "But it's military. Closed to the public."

"I'm not the public. I'm a journalist," I countered.

"I'll see what I can do."

My friend put me in touch with another military friend, a colonel, who had some influence.

While I was still in Delhi I called him and said, "I'll be in Leh tomorrow. Can I see you?"

The next morning I arrived on the dawn flight to Ladakh's capital Leh, found out that my cell phone didn't work, eventually found a phone in my hotel (intriguingly named The Yak Tail), and called the colonel, whom I hoped would be my savior.

"What? You're in Leh? I say, bad planning. I'm in Delhi," he said, once again showing how two people can be separated by a common language. "Not good at all. I need to get your passport, and get permission, and ..."

So I went directly to the course, spoke to the soldier in charge, and wrote a note to an even more senior officer based locally, who apparently had the power to grant me access. In the meantime I strolled around the course, which lies just a drive and five-iron from a street of shops.

Next to the first tee, named Sher Shah Suri after the fifteenth-century Moghul "Lion King," is a signboard reading: "Built 1967 as Trishul Golf Course, renamed Fire and Fury in 1999. 18 holes, 7,231 yards, par 72." Nothing about restricted access.

I stood on the elevated tee box, a room-sized construction rising about a meter off the ground. It was covered with dried mud, and in the center was a pizza-sized patch of scraggly grass, a golf course equivalent of Yasser Arafat's three-day stubble. Those few blades were about the only green found anywhere on the course. I later learned that most golfers carry their own little mats with them to use on the tees.

Just next to the first tee was the green for the 10th-hole, dubbed "10 Downing Street." It wasn't too hard to see that the course was maintained by the army corps of engineers – this particular green was perfectly square, and the bunker next to it was perfectly rectangular.

Actually the green wasn't green. It was black. I studied the substance – motor oil mixed with sand. A ball rolled more or less true, but slowly.

I walked around the course. In one section several gardeners were planting some five hundred willow trees to provide what, I'm not too sure – a golfing challenge? A touch of green? A practical horticultural exercise in drip irrigation?

Ladakh is mostly a high-altitude desert, and even though the region had a snowy winter, during my early-spring visit the golf course appeared lunar and severe, brown and unwelcoming. It's set in a bowl, about the size of New York's Central Park, with stunning views of the Khardang Mountains. I could see the road winding up to the Khardang-la pass, at 5,603 meters the world's highest motorable road.

Obviously, this is high country, populated by ethnic Tibetans who sometimes appear closer to the secrets of the cosmos than flat-dwellers.

IS FIRE AND FURY THE WORLD'S HIGHEST GOLF COURSE?

The Tuctu Golf Club in Peru, high in the Andes at 4,335 meters, once held the record, but it was abandoned over a decade ago and is now, according to one report, an unplayable mass of bush and vegetation.

With Tuctu out of action, Ladakh's Fire and Fury is certainly the highest eighteen-hole golf course in the world, at 3,445 meters. Next comes La Paz Golf Club in Bolivia, at 3,292 meters, which can stake a claim to be the highest *grass* course in the world.

By comparison, the highest United States courses are non-contenders in the nosebleed sweepstakes. Mount Massive, a nine-hole course in Leadville, Colorado, claims to be the highest course in North America at 2,950 meters, but the highest eighteen-hole course is Copper Creek Golf Club at Copper Mountain, also in Colorado. Its clubhouse, the location where official altitude is determined, is at 2,895 meters, but portions of the course climb to 2,956 meters.

I EVENTUALLY MET SOME HIGH-RANKING OFFICERS AT THE military barracks in Leh. Their responses were similar:

"Too bad you're here for such a short time, we'd love to play with you, but you have to get an intelligence clearance."

"But it's a golf course," I argued.

"Yes, but it's also a military training area."

Ladakh occupies a strategic position – the territory is scrunched between perennial enemies Pakistan (the countries have fought three bitter wars since 1947) and China (a border war in 1962), making it a geopolitical hotspot. I saw that the military commanders weren't going to bend to make a middle-aged American writer happy.

So I pursued an alternative path and consulted Venerable Nawang Luto, a monk at the nearby Spituk monastery, whom I had befriended in 1979.

He listened to my tale and, with the wisdom of decades of Tibetan meditation behind him, basically said, "I can pray for your soul but the army is out of my control."

Nevertheless, I'm optimistic that if I return to Ladakh I will be granted permission to play Fire and Fury. I've already got my talisman – a bright blue golf cap bearing the Fire and Fury logo. Not taking any chances, I also acquired a prayer wheel that sends entreaties toward the heavens. So even if I don't get to play the course in this lifetime, I can perhaps take solace in the philosophy of my monk friend Nawang Luto. Existence is *skaywa*, a cycle, and if things don't work out in this life, there will always be another opportunity in another lifetime to play the gravel course at Fire and Fury. In the meantime I'm breathing deeply and practicing my shots off dirt.

Yeti lovers at Ogyen Choling. Fable? Reality?
Dark side of the soul? A romance for the ages?

ON THE YETI TRAIL

Chasing a wisp, a legend, a key to who we are.

OGYEN CHOLING, TANG VALLEY, BHUTAN

"f you want to look for a yeti, just climb the mountain behind the village. That's where they've been sighted."

I was enjoying a post-dinner whiskey with Kunzang Choden and her husband Walter Roder, at their home in the Tang Valley in central Bhutan. The talk had drifted into yeti tales. Kunzang's comment that yetis "have been sighted," caused me to pause. The logical part of my brain remembered the days when I was a teenager on a modest allowance buying Roman coins. Some dealers offered bulk lots of a hundred battered coins, with the tantalizing salesman's come-on, "gold has been found in lots like this." Plus the admonition: *Just climb that mountain.* It was a refrain I've heard elsewhere in Asia; when I was searching for tiger magicians, Hanuman's mountain, or small people of the forest, I was frequently told, "you can find the strange wonders you're searching for over the next hill, beyond the next mountain." *Just keep walking, just keep dreaming.*

On the other hand, this was Bhutan, a Himalayan country with a cultural mythology as rich as the biodiversity in its extensive forests. Bhutan is prime yeti habitat. Kunzang herself, who grew up in this rural valley, wrote a book titled *Bhutanese Tales of the Yeti*, so she has both local knowledge of things that go bump in the night as well as a Western logical education to help her put strange happenings into perspective.

I NEEDED A LONG, HARD WALK.

For the past several days, I had been helping my wife photograph temple murals for her Master's dissertation at Kunzang Choden's Ogyen Choling estate. My eyes were beginning to spin with images of bodhisattvas with unpronounceable names and convoluted mythologies. I don't know how Monique got them organized in her head. She pointed out rich and complex paintings of the eighty-four Mahasiddhas, tantric masters whose numbers include gurus with evocative descriptors like The Lotus-Born Brahmin, the Celibate Bell-Ringer, the Avaricious Hermit, the Peasant Guru, and the Elder Severed-Headed Sister. On one wall we admired the image of Padmasambhava, also known as Guru Rinpoche, who brought tantric Buddhism to Tibet; on another panel Sangay Menlha, the Medicine Buddha; and nearby a dramatic image of Avalokiteshvara, the bodhisattva of compassion, who changes form and gender to become the female Kuan-yin in the Chinese pantheon.

And then there was a rare mandala of Shambhala, the mythical "pure land" – I could see how an adept could reach a higher plane by meditating on the painting's spiritual geometry. Always hope for a better tomorrow, provided you believe strongly enough today.

So many tales, so many Big Ideas in this holy place.

Some of the pictures were hard to photograph – the light was a mixture of harsh sunlight mixed with deep shadow, with the added complication of irregularly placed overhead fluorescent lights. Also, some of the smaller images were hidden behind curtains or in dark corners, and could only be photographed by setting up a makeshift scaffold and light, painting the small area to be photographed. We estimated we had looked carefully at perhaps half of the painted images that needed to be catalogued. Each day brought a surprise; it was like looking at the world's biggest "Where's Waldo" illustration, or really paying attention to Hieronymus Bosch's "Garden of Earthly Delights."

TO A CASUAL OBSERVER THE TEMPLE WAS A MAGICAL, almost overwhelming series of rooms. But to a believer here in central Bhutan, these paintings provided teachings and moral guidance and cultural foundations that were beyond my comprehension. These weren't formal Western-style portraits. They were fantasies of color and metaphor and detail. No doubt hidden treasures still lurked to be deciphered and brought to light. After all, one of the temple's most prominent murals was devoted to Dorje Lingpa, the fourteenth century "treasure hunter" who was a founder of Ogyen Choling. This panel is so important and complex that Monique wrote an entire thesis analyzing the myriad of symbols of this single representation – of a man who had the sacred ability to discover physical ritual objects as well as philosophical truths that had been hidden by earlier saints, in anticipation of the arrival of a wise man like Dorje Lingpa. Perhaps the mural is telling us that each person is a "treasure hunter." Some might seek gold or fame. Others might seek revelations or wisdom. Or perhaps a wayward treasure hunter might even seek a creature like the yeti?

I SUFFER FROM STENDHAL'S SYNDROME – I GET A headache after spending too much time in the presence of overwhelmingly beautiful and important artwork. I needed some fresh air, broader horizons. A search for my own obscure treasures. Some yeti-hunting, a tough walk "up the mountain," was just what I wanted.

WHAT IS THE ALLURE OF A MIRAGE, OF A WISP, OF A legend?

Why are people so fascinated by the yeti?

Is it because they mirror our dark side, and in the process help define us as human?

KUNZANG GAVE ME A CRASH COURSE IN YETI-OLOGY.

"There are countless stories about the *megoi*," she said, using the Bhutanese name for the yeti.

They're not people.

They're not animals.

They're deities and spirits that can manifest as yetis, creatures with supernatural powers.

They are territorial and don't like intruders in their wilderness domain.

They can be dangerous. Or not.

They can make themselves invisible.

"Oh, there's one other distinctive feature. The females always have droopy breasts. They flip them over their shoulders when they run."

THERE IS A FEARSOME DROOPY-BREASTED JEWISH YETI, called Yetty in the local folklore.

One day in Florida, a withered grandmother named Yetty was walking along the beach with her young grandson. Suddenly a tidal wave appeared and swept the boy away. Yetty ranted and raved at her god; she begged and pleaded, cajoled and even prayed. "I've been a good woman, and he's just an innocent boy. Return him to me."

And out of the sea another tidal wave came, and she watched as the child, perched on top of the wave of water, was gently placed back on the shore next to her. Yetty was overjoyed, but after examining the boy she quickly became agitated. Waving her fists she shouted at the sky: "He had a hat!"

I STOPPED BY THE OGYEN CHOLING TEMPLE TO SEE how my new best friend Lhamola was getting on and to give him a gift.

Lhamola says he's ninety-six; Kunzang remembers that he was already a grown man when she was a girl, teasing the kids with ghost stories and leading them on adventures in the nearby hills. His hearing is pretty much gone. All the time we had been working in the temple, Lhamola sat by the window, wrapped in a blanket, chanting from the one hundred and eight volumes of the Kanjur, the Tibetan Buddhist holy scriptures. Such an act of devotion, which in Lhamola's case will take a year, brings great merit. Each book was constructed with accordion-like pages as long as his arm, covered in elegant Tibetan script. Each volume weighed about ten kilograms, and sometimes I would help Lhamola lift a just-completed book onto the shelf where they were kept, and help him take down another.

A similarly ancient lady from the village brought him some food, which he ignored as he continued his chanting. He paid us little attention. Days earlier I had asked Kunzang whether he knew what he was reading.

"He can hardly see," she replied. Just before we set off up the mountain in search of a yeti, I gave Lhamola a pair of purple-framed reading glasses. They seemed to suit him.

IN POPULAR WESTERN CULTURE, NEPAL GETS MOST OF the yeti media coverage. But Bhutan can also stake its claim to being a yeti stronghold.

Hearty trekkers can tackle the difficult "Snowman Trek" in the north of the country. This is an adventure I probably could have done twenty years ago, but my sell-by date has passed for this particular exploit.

And Bhutan is the only country that has created a national park to protect the yeti. This *is* a place in which I have trekked, the Merak-Sakteng National Park in the east of the country. Good people, lovely scenery, not a yeti in sight.

FOR THE CLIMB TO THE "YETI-SIGHTING PLACE," AT A location called Khramai, I was accompanied by our guide Karma Wangdi, 61, and a local farmer named Tashi Phuntso, 39. After about an hour of setting off, Phuntso's dog Norsangla decided to join us. Phuntso had left him behind, but Norsangla, 4, obviously had felt that he wanted to be part of our adventure.

The path kept climbing. I stopped a few times to take

some deep breaths of the air, as pellucid as air can be, air that has never come in close contact with industry or cars or rock concerts. For Tashi Phuntso it was a walk in the park. For Karma Wangdi it was a workout, for although a village boy who grew up in an adjacent valley, he has lived years in the cushier environment of Thimphu, Bhutan's capital. For me it was a boy's adventure. About halfway up I could see our destination, a large building perched on the edge of an outcrop. It didn't look that far away.

TASHI PHUNTSO, OUR VILLAGE GUIDE, HAD STREET-CRED. He said he had seen a *megoi* a few years earlier. It was a rainy morning and he had gone to help his mother care for the yak herd. Lingering nearby was a *megoi*, who sauntered off when it saw Phuntso approach. Phuntso showed us the field where the encounter had taken place.

I HAD NEVER MET A VILLAGE DOG AS ZEN-LIKE AS Norsangla. He's a big, black and tan mountain dog, with one brown eye, one blue. Most Bhutanese village dogs are fierce. Norsangla, whose name means "good wishes," never barked. He was as gentle as a suburban golden retriever. He was tactile and liked to have the back of his ears scratched. I dare say, his was an "old soul."

But I wasn't sure that having Norsangla around was

good for our yeti search. If a yeti came calling, would Norsangla break his silence and scare off the yeti? Or would the yeti sense that this placid animal was an easy midnight snack and invade our camp?

THERE ARE TWO SCHOOLS OF THOUGHT ABOUT WHAT entices/disgusts a yeti. "To attract a yeti, burn plastic and rubbish," Kunzang said. "They are sensitive to bad smells and will become angry that someone is polluting their neighborhood and come to investigate."

I liked the idea of an eco-conscious yeti, but other folks told me the opposite.

"No, better to burn sweet-smelling pine, juniper, and herbs," Karma said. He had accompanied us from Thimphu but grew up on a farm in an adjacent valley. "They are attracted to homely, natural smells."

Ditto for personal hygiene. One expert said I should not bathe and must hang around barnyard yaks for a few days. Another self-declared expert, however, recommended deodorant and flossing.

THE BIGGEST QUANDARY POTENTIALLY FACED BY A YETI-hunter is, *what do you do if you find one?*

A true scientist would say that's no quandary at all. You hit it with a tranquillizer dart and do the needful. No tranquilizer gun? Well, you shoot the thing. Because unless you have one on the lab table, all you have is a Grand Wisp of Lofty Expectations.

But most yeti-chasers wouldn't pull the trigger.

I attribute this reticence to two concerns.

The first is that the yeti is so close to being human that killing one would be a form of homicide.

The second is that most yeti-chasers don't actually want the animal to be found. They don't want the yeti to be autopsied, to have its skull measured, its hair and blood analyzed, its stools picked through, its DNA put through an expensive techno-gadget that would tell us how close the animal is to us, and vice versa. Most serious yeti-chasers claim they prefer to live with the myth, although my cynical side feels that this "keep-the-myth-alive" attitude might simply be the rationalization of researchers who failed in capturing the beast.

PEOPLE STRIVE FOR THE LIGHT. MOTHS TO THE FLAME and all that.

But even the brightest, most enlightened individual has a shadow.

Our dark side – depressive, violent, arrogant, spiteful, fearful – is something we try to overcome. Some people seek religion. Some turn to meditation. Others engage in merit-making and doing good works. And some people couldn't give a damn and carry on, business as usual.

Jung called this dark side of the soul the "shadow."

Some Asian religions call this "ignorance," and temples and morality tales are rich in illustrating the idea that one of the main job descriptions of the gods, and hence of mortal men, is to subdue the deformed Dwarf of Ignorance.

Do yeti stories evolve from this recognition of the duality of the soul? So much Asian philosophy is based on managing opposites. To get crops to grow you need both the rainy season and the sunny season. There is the cycle of life and death. The world runs on an endless dynamic of polarities: male and female, exploration and nurturing, day and night, good and evil.

The Balinese, who (with some justification) consider themselves a highly evolved society, file the cuspids of boys and girls so that the children do not have "animal teeth." In other parts of Indonesia, babies are not allowed to crawl on the floor, lest they develop animal-like characteristics. No matter how poor you are, you make an effort to be presentable, with good (or at least clean) clothes and socially approved deportment. No wonder many traditionally educated Asians shake their heads when they encounter loud, rude Westerners. Asians can be both appalled and curious when they see men who wear backward baseball caps and put their shoe-encased feet on beds and furniture. And let's not mention what emotions are stirred when Asians see Western women who wear ridiculous outfits when they go to Walmart. (Though to be fair, plenty of contemporary Asians take rudeness and bad behavior to impressive levels; arrogance and bad manners are not the sole domain of Westerners. A curse on all their ill-mannered houses.)

The yeti is not human. But it's a disturbingly close reverse image, like looking at ourselves in a darkened mirror. The yeti is Caliban, close enough to ourselves to make us wonder what this business we call humanity is all about.

You define yourself partly by what you are not.

As W.B. Yeats wrote in "The Second Coming":

Turning and turning in the widening gyre
The falcon cannot hear the falconer
Things fall apart; the centre cannot hold;
Mere anarchy is loosed upon the world,
The blood-dimmed tide is loosed, and everywhere
The ceremony of innocence is drowned.
The best lack all conviction, while the worst
Are full of passionate intensity.

WHAT DO WE MAKE OF THE TALE OF XU YUNBAO, WHO was photographed before he died in 1962 and whose corpse was exhumed and examined in 1980. UPI reported:

Born to a peasant woman in central Sichuan province [China] in 1939, his body was covered with hair and he was bent at the waist. He grew to a height of only three feet and used all four limbs when walking. Xu refused clothing even during winter and lived on a diet of raw corn, vehemently rejecting cooked food. His brain capacity never grew over 350 ml [an average man has a brain capacity of 1,200 to 1,500 ml] and his spinal column and limbs were even more backward in construction than those of the Peking Man who lived more than 400,000 years ago. His skull, which shows the primitive characteristics of man's ancestors hundreds of thousands of years ago, was only eight centimeters in diameter at birth.

Xu resembles the prehistoric ancestors we are trying to disinherit from our consciousness. The description of him locked away in a tiny village causes the same emotional reaction we might have to capturing a yeti and putting it on display, or shooting one and filing it away in a specimen drawer at a museum. Catching a yeti might be a remarkable achievement for science, but it might also be a low point for humanity. Perhaps it is better that the yeti not be discovered.

COULD THE "WILD MEN" HAVE AN ATAVISTIC LINK WITH wild beasts encountered when our pre-human ancestors overlapped with other collateral hominids?

Harry Marshall, a British filmmaker who has made documentaries on the yeti, *orang pendek*, and related creatures for BBC and *National Geographic*, says:

We know that our Homo sapiens ancestors overlapped with other hominids, that they mated and produced viable offspring, of which we are the proof. Our genome, with its small but significant percentages of Neanderthal and Denisovan (and who knows what else) DNA is evidence of this hybridization. I believe the parable of Esau and Jacob – the smooth man and the hairy man – is an allegory of how our ancestors usurped the birthright – or more simply, ethnically cleansed their world of the other hominids we once shared the planet with. I think it's an extraordinary part of who we are and genetics is finally going to reveal the extent of our involvement with and debt to the hairy other.

MYTHS AND LEGENDS OF GIANTS AND APE-MEN HAVE survival value for mankind – we need to be reminded of what our life might be like if we did not have culture, that uniquely human attribute. As the British primatologist John Napier suggests, humans need to experience feelings of awe.

Husbands, fathers, elders, statesmen, dictators, presidents, chairmen and grand masters are all very well as god-figures, but they are inadequate because they lack the essential ingredient of remoteness. Man needs his gods – and his monsters – and the more remote and unapproachable they are, the better.

The yeti may or may not exist in reality. But there is no question that it has an eternal home in the human spirit.

I TOOK ANOTHER REST BREAK AS WE CLIMBED UP THE "yetis-have-been-sighted" mountain. I munched a Snickers. I was tired, to be sure, but my modest efforts couldn't compare with the travails of serious yeti-hunters, like my friend Jeffrey McNeely.

DURING A TWO-YEAR STINT IN THE MOUNTAINS OF eastern Nepal, conservationist McNeely found yeti spoor at his team's study site between Mount Everest and Mount Kanchenjunga, some two-weeks walk from the nearest road.

The first evidence was a large human-like stool near the camp that McNeely at first thought came from one of the porters. But the stool included chunks of partly digested bone and hair, perhaps from a serow, a Himalayan antelope.

Then one December morning, McNeely and his colleagues woke to find distinctive footprints in the fresh snow around their tents. "They were about an American size 12 [European size 45], and quite wide. Our first thought was that they might be footprints of a bear," McNeely, co-author of *Mammals of Thailand*, said. "But no; these had a round heel while bears have a pointed heel, and there were no claw marks, which would have been present if it had been a bear."

They followed the footprints for a couple hundred meters, until the tracks disappeared into a gulch.

McNeely took some photos and made plaster casts of

the footprints. He asked a friend, Andrew Laurie, to carry them out of the country to Bangkok, where McNeely and his colleagues lived.

The casts were carefully packed in an aluminum case, which Laurie, who had been studying Indian rhinos in the Chitwan area of Nepal, carried as hand luggage. At the airport security screening, he was asked what he was carrying, and he explained that they were plaster casts of animals.

"Yeti?" asked the Nepalese customs inspector?

"Er, yes," Laurie replied.

"In that case they're a national treasure," the customs man said, confiscating the case and its contents. They were never seen again.

I ASKED MCNEELY WHAT HE THOUGHT HE HAD DISCOVERED.

McNeely is a good friend, whose comments sometimes verge on the cynical. He's a pragmatic scientist who isn't afraid to speculate on what *might be*. The absence of proof does not mean proof of absence.

"I can't confirm it was a yeti," he said. "But I hold out hope it might be."

I suggested that the never-ending search for the yeti would only be solved one way or another if someone captured an animal.

"You're right," he said, "but I hope it's never found."

"But you believe in the yeti?" As I said it I realized it sounded like a religious question.

He caught my drift and replied, "The local people certainly believe it." And then my American friend gave a Gallic-type shrug, as if to say, "Who knows?"

THE WALK TO KHRAMAI TURNED OUT TO BE FARTHER, and harder, than I had anticipated. We gained about a thousand meters in elevation to reach an altitude of forty-two hundred meters. We finally came upon a substantial two-level house, framed by wild rhododendrons beginning to bud. I marveled at the skill of Bhutanese carpenters to build big, sturdy structures in unlikely places. The bottom level was devoid of furniture but dry and moderately clean. The upper floor contained a small chapel, still in use by passing yak-herders. No doubt it would shelter people and their spirits through rude winters.

Our home for the night was built about a hundred years ago by a Tibetan monk who lived in the village just below Ogyen Choling. The timing of its construction coincided with the age of the temple murals my wife was studying. It's a long shot, but could the murals in the "yeti-sighting place" chapel have been painted by the same artisan who painted the chapel Monique was studying in Ogyen Choling?

MY NIGHT AT KHRAMAI PASSED UNEVENTFULLY, AS I expected. No gentle owl-like "hoo-hoo" sounds that would have signaled that a yeti was up and about. I slept peacefully, as did Norsangla. The fire burned until about ten at night, fragrant with juniper smoke. After that we were alone with the stars and wind that rippled the prayer flags.

I WASN'T DISAPPOINTED AT NOT HAVING A YETI sighting because I hadn't expected one.

We returned to Ogyen Choling around midday. "Any luck?" Kunzang asked as we shared a quick bite of lunch. I laughed and shook my head.

Kunzang and I then wandered over to the temple to see what my wife was getting up to.

Monique was with Karma, our guide who had just accompanied me on the yeti trek.

"Look what we found!" Monique said. She parted a curtain above a dark doorway. I didn't see anything. "Look with the flashlight," she instructed and I saw a painting, about fifteen centimeters high, of two long-haired, human-like creatures. They formed a couple, and the male had his arm around the female, who had long droopy breasts.

"It's a yeti!" Karma said.

My ancient friend Lhamola paid little attention to the exuberance going on around him and continued his chanting.

"I grew up here; I've used this temple since I was a little girl, and I never saw this," Kunzang said. She called for her husband.

Walter ran in, thinking someone had been injured. "Look at what Monique and Karma found!" Kunzang said.

Karma's comment was more prosaic. "We didn't have to hike up the mountain to find a yeti. We've got one right here."

ABOUT THE AUTHOR

Paul with his Flying *Zizi* from Bhutan.

PAUL SPENCER SOCHACZEWSKI has written *Share Your Journey, An Inordinate Fondness for Beetles, The Sultan and the Mermaid Queen, Redheads, Soul of the Tiger* (co-authored with Jeff McNeely), and other acclaimed books, along with some six hundred bylined articles in leading international publications. He has lived and worked in more than eighty countries, including long stints in Southeast Asia.

Visit Paul at:
www.sochaczewski.com

Praise for

PAUL'S OTHER BOOKS

SHARE YOUR JOURNEY:
MASTERING PERSONAL WRITING
ISBN: 978-2-940573-15-8

"*Share Your Journey* is to good writing as *Joy of Cooking* is to good food. I wish all my students had this book before taking my writing classes; hell, I wish I had this book earlier in my career. It's smart, fun, and every page contains nuggets of essential advice."

—GARY GOSHGARIAN, professor, Northeastern University;
as Gary Braver, award-winning author of *Tunnel Vision*

"As publisher of Moon Publications for 17 years, I worked with scores of writers to produce award-winning guide-books to countries and regions around the world. *Share Your Journey* is an invaluable aid to all writers wishing to discover their voices and effectively connect to their readers."

—BILL DALTON, author of *Indonesia Handbook*

"I had just completed a new book. I was pleased with it, until I read *Share Your Journey* and realized how I could make it better. Many writing guides turn what should be a liberating experience into drudgery and scolding rules. *Share Your Journey* is different; it helps you unleash an inner voice you may not have realized was inside you. It's also great fun. As a writer of fiction and biography infused with personal travel, I appreciate its originality and power. I wish many of the fellow writers I review would adapt its suggestions!"

—NIGEL BARLEY, author of *Island of Dreams*, *White Rajah* and *In the Footsteps of Stamford Raffles*

"Paul Sochaczewski learned his craft slowly and carefully over a period of decades, and he now shares the secrets to why he's successful in a book. He offers ten simple and obvious, but too often overlooked guidelines, then amply illustrates each with samples from his own works and a library full of other writers (many of them household names), demonstrating how easily it can be done."

—JERRY HOPKINS, former editor of *Rolling Stone* and best-selling author of *No One Gets Out of Here Alive*, *Bangkok Babylon*, *Elvis: The Biography*, and *Romancing the East*

"If you want to write, if you want to improve your writing, if you want your writing to leap off the page and click its heels in midair, read this book and follow its good advice. This is a lifetime's wisdom, offered by a pro."

—THOMAS BASS, author of *The Spy Who Loved Us*, *Vietnamerica*, and *The Predictors*; professor of English and journalism at State University of New York

"Before I became a journalist, Paul had shown me how to write a convincing personal travel piece, something that both tells a good story and connects well with the reader. This was a breakthrough for me: The resulting article, about a quirky Indonesian theater group, led to my first appearance in the major mainline press – the *Wall Street Journal*. His good advice helped place this piece, which in turn helped me land a foreign correspondent's position in Asia with a Dow Jones-owned newsweekly. I'm delighted that Paul's wisdom and sense of humor animate his new book, *Share Your Journey*. Many major writers have offered advice – think of John Steinbeck, William Safire, or George Orwell; Paul's Ten Tips, buttressed by some great to-the-point examples, will stand among the best advice a non-fiction writer can ever hope to have."

—JAMES CLAD, former professor at Georgetown University and Johns Hopkins University; former Far Eastern Economic Review bureau chief in Malaysia, India, and the Philippines; former U.S. assistant secretary of defense; author of *Behind the Myth: Business, Money and Power in Southeast Asia*

"If I had to parachute only one book to a Robinson Crusoe-type stranded on a desert island who wanted to write his personal story, I have no doubt it would be Paul Sochaczewski's *Share Your Journey: Mastering Personal Writing*. The toolkit Paul offers allows the person with a story and some raw talent to build a word castle that rises to the heavens."

—CHRISTOPHER G. MOORE, author of the Vincent Calvino novels and *Heart Talk*

AN INORDINATE FONDNESS FOR BEETLES
ISBN: 978-981-4385-20-6

"A natural storyteller, Paul Sochaczewski has created something much bigger than an "in the footsteps of" book. He has produced a work that looks at the themes Wallace wrote about and lived through – women's power, why boys leave home, the need to collect, our relation with other species, nature destruction, arrogance, the role of ego, white-brown and brown-brown colonialism, serendipity, passion, mysticism – and interpreted them through his own filter. He is a gifted storyteller and the layers of thought, humor, history, commentary, and outrageousness Sochaczewski has given us provides a very special view of Wallace that goes beyond biography, beyond travelogue, beyond memoir."

—DANIEL NAVID, international environment and development law expert; former UN diplomat and founding secretary general of the International Wetlands Convention

"This is a classic hero's journey – actually a double hero's journey – which amuses, entertains and surprises us as Wallace and Sochaczewski both experience life-changing adventures in Southeast Asia. Wallace was one of science's great overachievers, and by following his trail, Sochaczewski explores, with ample wit and sardonic insight, Wallace's extraordinary breakthrough in 19th-century evolutionary thinking, and reveals how this relates to contemporary Southeast Asian society, politics, and the conservation of life on earth."

—ANDREW W. MITCHELL, founder and director, Global Canopy Programme; author of *The Enchanted Canopy*

"A new category of nonfiction – part personal travelogue, part incisive biography of Wallace, part unexpected travel-ler's tales that coalesce into an illuminating, sometimes bizarre, and always-entertaining volume."

—JEFFREY SAYER, professor of Conservation and Development, James Cook University; founding director general, Centre for International Forestry Research

"Sochaczewski is an explorer of ideas and issues that Wallace cared about deeply: the natural dignity of tribal peoples, the role of colonialism, threats to our natural environment, why boys leave home to seek adventures and collect, how women will determine mankind's future, and how difficult it is to eliminate ego and greed from people in positions of power."

—ROBIN HANBURY-TENISON, explorer; author of *Mulu: The Rainforest*, *The Oxford Book of Exploration*, and *The Great Explorers*

"Untypeable – not solely either travel or history or biography or memoir or essay, but all in its turn, overflows with enthusiasm and respect for Wallace. A volume of parallel adventures, a subtle work, subtly and artfully structured. Wallace and Sochaczewski invite the reader to join in and make a threesome."

—OTTO STEINMEYER, Borneo Research Bulletin

"A fascinating journey through the tropics of Southeast Asia, Sochaczewski not only follows in the footsteps of Alfred Russel Wallace, but engages in a dialog with him for the whole journey. Thought-provoking about change and constancy, and a delight to read."

—PETER H. RAVEN, president emeritus,
Missouri Botanical Garden

"*An Inordinate Fondness for Beetles* has the rhythm and magic of a verbal fugue. Words, phrases, and even whole passages recur, focusing the reader back from lively diversions to the central theme. Two minds, moulded by contrasting background and upbringing, are reflected in reaction to people and places of the region, geographically linked but chronologically divided. Neither man eschews controversy, nor hesitates to express an opinion on current policies and events. Read, laugh and, in the light of impacts during the past century and a half, ponder with Sochaczewski on the uncertain future of the people and the wildlife of land and sea in this gloriously biodiverse archipelago."

—DATO SRI GATHORNE, Earl of Cranbrook;
author of *Mammals of Borneo*, *Mammals of Southeast Asia*, and
Wonders of the Natural World of Southeast Asia

THE SULTAN AND THE MERMAID QUEEN
ISBN: 978-981-4217-74-3

"Sochaczewski is blessed with a relentlessly probing curiosity, an easy-to-read writing style, and a sensitive soul. His explorations of the remote jungles, far-flung archipelagoes, and quirky characters of Asia leave us with fascinating accounts that mix natural history and modern-day reporting to investigate old fables and inspire new ones."

—JAMES FAHN, author of *A Land on Fire: The Environmental Consequences of the Southeast Asian Boom*; executive director of the Earth Journalism Network

"A wonderful book about traditions and beliefs in Asia. Sochaczewski has that rare gift to bring history and fable to life with respect and affection. This book should be required reading for politicians and people in NGOs concerned with Asia – indeed for anyone seeking a better understanding of life and culture in this most fascinating part of the world."

—DANIEL NAVID, international environment and development law expert; former UN diplomat and secretary general of the International Wetlands Convention

"Sochaczewski is a knowledgeable guide to an often obscure world, revealing Asian cultures often themselves on the brink of extinction. In a hundred years, books like *The Sultan and the Mermaid Queen* may be our only reference to belief systems and a way of life that have gone extinct."

—CHRISTOPHER G. MOORE,
author of the Vincent Calvino novels and *Heart Talk*

"This is travel writing with a quirky difference. Admirers of Paul Spencer Sochaczewski's serio-comic novel *Redheads*, set in the jungles of Borneo, will already know him as a dedicated environmentalist with a taste for offbeat characters and exotic settings. This collection of personal essays introduces a fascinating collection of real-life figures, ranging from a homeless man in Hawaii who claims to be the true last emperor of China to a group of Burmese monks who have trained cats to perform acrobatic tricks."

—WILLIAM WARREN, author of *Jim Thompson: The Unsolved Mystery* and *The Tropical Garden*

"Having grown up in Asia, I am deeply indebted to Paul Sochaczewski for his unique ability to reawaken the memories of the humanity and humor, wonder and reality of this magical part of the world. These stories leap off the pages and head straight into your heart. *The Sultan and the Mermaid Queen* is one of the finest gifts you could possibly give to yourself and to your best friends."

—ANDY SUNDBERG, United States presidential candidate (1988);
former worldwide chairman of Democrats Abroad;
founder, American Citizens Abroad; U.S. Naval officer;
co-founder of Burlamaqui Society

"For three decades Paul Sochaczewski has been trawling Asia for lost white tribes, Hobbits, dancing ghosts, the Last Emperor of China, and dancing temple cats, reporting back with tales of hilarity and insight. He's also been at the forefront of efforts to raise awareness of Asia's great environmental diversity, documenting the struggle of indigenous tribes in Borneo to save their precious forest, and has championed 'Darwin's shadow,' that other great of evolution, Alfred Russel Wallace. This collection captures the diversity of Asia in all its colorful, and often funny, glory."

—JOHN CLEWLEY, *Bangkok Post* columnist

"Only a lifetime of ambling through Asian cultures could enrich a writer to this degree and enable him to infuse his writing with local lore and wisdom in the manner Paul Sochaczewski has done in this colorful and insightful collection."

—JOHN EVERINGHAM, photographer; publisher: Artasia Press,
Dragon Art Media

"As a mystic healer I understand the spiritual power of the Mermaid Queen, and have on occasion merged with her strong presence. In this book Sochaczewski has managed something quite extraordinary – he has taken exotic, sometimes esoteric subjects and made them interesting and accessible. His writing peels back the layers of myth and reality, revealing a sensitive, humorous, and insightful core of humanity."

—AMA LIA WAI-CHING LEE, Pemangku Maha Jeroh Sandat;
mystic healer; dancer; chronicler

REDHEADS
ISBN 0-9587448-9-0

"*Redheads* does for the struggle to save the rainforests of Borneo what *Catch 22* did for the struggle to stay alive in World War II."

—DANIEL QUINN, author of *Ishmael*

"*Redheads* is a roaring tale of tropical suspense, an eco-thriller that is witty and smart and altogether a wonderful treat. It is the perfect example of a new genre, an eco-thriller so suspenseful that you learn about this strange world while sitting on the edge of your seat."

—THOMAS BASS, author of *The Predictors* and *Camping with the Prince and Other Tales of Science in Africa*

"A fast-paced novel, at once very funny and deeply serious, about a subject that should be of concern to everyone in today's world."

—WILLIAM WARREN, author of *Jim Thompson: The Legendary American of Thailand*

"An absorbing story, reminiscent of the social commentary of Somerset Maugham and Evelyn Waugh. Everyone working in conservation should read it and heed it."

—JIM THORSELL, senior advisor, World Heritage, IUCN

"*Redheads* is a terrific book about apes and people, do-gooders and do-baddders, science and superstition, ecology and psychology, nature and nurture, and how we all fit together in this old world."

—MARK OLSHAKER, author of *The Edge*; co-author of *Mindhunter*

"A ribald, engrossing novel with a deeper message regarding the clash of cultures and our relation to the environment."

—EDWIN BERNBAUM, author of *Sacred Mountains of the World*

"*Redheads* combines the witty insights of George MacDonald Fraser with the realism of Thomas Hardy – a real Asian treat."

—JEFFREY A. MCNEELY, chief scientist,
IUCN – The World Conservation Union

"This rambunctious romp through the Borneo jungles is both fun and deceptively insightful. If this is how the world really works in the realm of nature protection, then where do we go from here? The story reveals important realities about the way things can be in the hurley-burley world of nature protection and environmentalism. Noble-intentioned jetsetting environmentalists: Take Heed!"

—SIR RUSSELL BETTS, former director of WWF – World Wide
Fund for Nature's Indonesian Program